Don't Graduate Clueless: Expert Advice To Help You Prepare For Success In Today's Economy

by Beth Campbell Duke

I0476236

Don't Graduate Clueless:

Expert Advice To Help You Prepare For Success In Today's Economy

Beth Campbell Duke
Copyright © 2015

Beth Campbell Duke
The Career Tutor
PO Box 101 Union Bay, BC Canada   V0R 3B0
Visit our website at http://TheCareerTutor.com

Limit of Liability/Disclaimer of Warranty

For general information on our other products and services or for technical support please contact Beth Campbell Duke; http://TheCareerTutor.com

First Edition: (June, 2015)

10 9 8 7 6 5 4 3 2 1

For Tony

Who is one of those self-employed people my parents
warned me about.

*"I learned that courage was not the absence
of fear, but the triumph over it. The brave
man is not he who does not feel afraid, but he
who conquers that fear."*

~ Nelson Mandela

Table of Contents

Your Free Gift

As a way of saying, 'Thank You' for purchasing this book, I'm offering 5 free interviews with some of the top career, education and small business experts I interviewed as research for this book.

During these interviews, we discussed much more than what made it to the book!

To get exclusive access to these bonus interviews, head over to:

http://TheCareerTutor.com/dont-graduate-clueless

Foreword: Our Experts

I am indebted beyond words to the people listed here – career, workplace and educational experts who generously gave of their time to answer my questions, share their expertise, and tell me about their own experiences with the changes we're all navigating 'out there' in the world of work. Thank you!

In their stories you'll see examples of how people are now more often using their life experiences to influence how they work and what they choose to do. We really are bringing more of who we are to our work.

One of the lessons I relearned from working on this interview-format book is that we really aren't alone. When you reach out for advice in your own work journey, know that you'll find it.

Rumeet Billan (RumeetBillan.com)

Rumeet is the President of Jobs in Education and teaches courses in Leadership and Social Entrepreneurship. She is completing her PhD at the University of Toronto and has been honored twice as one of Canada's Most Powerful Women. Her global initiatives include building schools in Africa and Central America, developing a Teacher Training Centre, and supporting projects that help support her vision of enabling opportunities in education.

Find Rumeet online at JobsInEducation.com, Twitter and *LinkedIn.* Watch Rumeet's *TEDxNovaScotiaEd* Talk.

Dick Bolles (JobHuntersBible.com)

Dick Bolles is the author of What Color Is Your Parachute? A Practical Guide For Job-Hunters and Career Changers, 2014, the most popular job-hunting book in the world.

The book has sold more than 10,000,000 copies to date, and is dramatically updated, reshaped and rewritten, every year, with the newest edition appearing mid-August each year, in bookstores or online. The 2014 edition is now available.

Find Dick online on Facebook and LinkedIn

Anita Bruzzese (45Things.com)

Anita Bruzzese is a nationally syndicated columnist on the workplace and award-winning journalist.

Also a highly rated speaker, she has addressed audiences on topics ranging from taking control of your career, avoiding workplace blunders and responsible business blogging.

She has appeared on The Today show, been interviewed on public radio and been quoted in many national publications such as O, The Oprah Magazine, Glamour and BusinessWeek.com.

Find Anita on Twitter and Linked In

Dr. Anne Davies (AnneDavies.com)

Dr. Davies balances her time between teaching, research and writing. She has worked in North America as well as Germany, New Zealand, Norway, Singapore, and UK. She is invited to work with a variety of countries, districts, organizations, schools and universities. For the past several years she has also been supporting learning via a variety of web institutes, conferences and online courses. Dr. Davies has completed more than 30 books and multi-media resources – many of them in collaboration with others.

"We must prepare all learners for their future, not our past."

Find Dr. Davies on LinkedIn

Scott Dinsmore (LiveYourLegend.net)

Imagine a world where everyone did work that made them come alive. Imagine if you were surrounded by the people who made that type of life possible.

What would that look like? How differently would you treat people? How much harder would you pursue the things in front of you? How would those around you start to treat others as a result of how you treated them?

One ripple creates another. When enough ripples intersect, we have a revolution.

Find Scott online on Facebook and Twitter. Watch Scott's TEDxGoldenGate Talk.

Lauren Friese (TalentEgg.ca)

TalentEgg was founded by Lauren Friese after she and many of her friends experienced difficulty transitioning from school to work. Upon graduating, Lauren wasn't sure exactly what to do next. Like many students, she opted for grad school, attending the London School of Economics in the UK.

There, she discovered, it was much easier to make the transition thanks to a number of career websites that allowed her to research job opportunities and browse free resources.

TalentEgg launched in April 2008, and is now the leader in online campus recruitment in Canada.

Find Lauren online on Twitter and LinkedIn

Kelly Green (ProfitableBusinessBrands.com)

Kelly spent 15 years as a marketing executive in the entertainment industry. But in 2005 it all came to an end due to a health challenge. She certified as a wellness coach and began a new career and a new life. The career change allowed Kelly to talk to people facing similar health challenges, and gave her the lifestyle she was looking for.

Kelly began to notice an underlying theme among most of her clients – they had lost their identity in their illness.

That's when it all clicked for her! Kelly was not only coaching my clients to make better lifestyle choices, she was teaching them the importance of developing and clarifying their Brand.

Find Kelly online on Facebook, LinkedIn and Twitter

Alexandra Levit (AlexandraLevit.com)

Alexandra Levit's goal is to help people succeed in meaningful jobs, and to build relationships between organizations and top talent. A former nationally syndicated columnist for the Wall Street Journal and a current writer for the New York Times, Alexandra has authored several books, including the bestselling They Don't Teach Corporate in College, How'd You Score That Gig?, Success for Hire, MillennialTweet, New Job, New You, and Blind Spots.

Alexandra produced the critically acclaimed JobSTART 101, a free online course that better prepares college students and graduates for the challenges of the workplace.

Find Alexandra online on LinkedIn and Twitter.

JT O'Donnell (Careerealism.com)

Jeanine Tanner "J.T." O'Donnell is a career strategist and workplace consultant who helps American workers of all ages find greater professional satisfaction.

O'Donnell's work has been cited in Wall Street Journal, USA Today, New York Times, The Boston Globe, CNN.com, MSNBC.com, AOL.com, Careerbuilder.com, BusinessWeek.com, Mashable.com, Yahoo.com and dozens of other national publications.

Her book, CAREEREALISM: The Smart Approach to a Satisfying Career, outlines her highly successful career-coaching methodology.

Find JT online on , LinkedIn and TwitterFacebook

Joshua Waldman (CareerEnlightenment.com)

When Joshua was laid off two times in six months back in 2008, he decided it was time to really understand the modern job search. By applying his knowledge of social media to proven job search strategies, he found himself winding up in the interview chair in a fraction of the time it took his peers.

But it was too soon for him after the layoffs. And so the only images in Joshua's head during the job interviews were pictures of getting laid off from yet another great company.

'Yep. I still had plenty of healing to do. So I decided that while I was recovering, I would help other people who were ready for the job. That's when I started Career Enlightenment, it was late 2009.'

Find Joshua online on Facebook, Twitter and LinkedIn

Dr. Michael 'Woody' Woodward (DrWoody.com)

As a consultant and professional coach, Dr. Woody works with both private and corporate clients on career development and building management/leadership capacity. As an author and speaker, Dr. Woody focuses on the psychology of career engagement in the New Economy and how to make the transition from "player" to "coach" (moving to the management and executive ranks) in the business world.

Dr. Woody published his first book The YOU Plan: A 5-step Guide to Taking Charge of Your Career in the New Economy (2nd edition out 5/2012) and he also writes a regular weekly column called The Career Hot Seat.

Find Michael on Facebook, Twitter and LinkedIn

Introduction

There's more attention on the struggle, on the pain, on the problem of how this country transitions young people from school into the workplace. ~Lauren Friese

I love Lauren's quote because although the recent changes in the economy and the world of work have caused significant struggle and pain, the great news is that we're paying more attention.

When I interviewed the experts for this book, I specifically asked them for advice they'd give to the parents of the students and (sometimes not-so-) recent grads they work with. The 'thing' is, the changes to the economy and labour market have been recent and massive - so the advice here is appropriate for everyone because we're all learning new skills in how to cope and create life/work success.

A Few Words To Parents Reading This Book - I frequently speak with frustrated parents who want to help their young adults with job hunting and career advice, but aren't sure how. I hope this book gives you some insight into the changes we've all experienced in the 'world of work', and the changes we haven't yet experienced in school-based career education.

The struggles our kids are facing are real.

If you're a Gen-Xer who's having to look for work 'out there', the struggles you're facing are real.

Unlike the career advice most of us had as youth, there IS decent advice available. Look for advisors who have experience with recent job search and career strategies.

A Few Words To Students & Recent Grads Reading This Book - Know 2 things:

1.   Parents and teachers want the best for you, even if they appear frustrated and seem to have outdated advice (in which case, you can show them this book), and

2.   Unlike the career advice your parents and teachers had, there IS decent advice available. Find an advisor or two who have experience with recent job search and career strategies. Unlike your parents' and teachers' generation - you're going to be looking for new work opportunities frequently over the course of your life. Think of it as a series of opportunities!

Don't Panic!

* * *

I'm either the youngest of the Boomer generation or the oldest of the Gen-Xers. I prefer to think of myself as among the oldest of Generation X. We're also known as the Nexus, or Sandwich Generation because we often find ourselves 'in-between' the discussions on generations. We have aging parents and (step-)children heading to college.

We grew up in a time of radical change - we're old enough to remember having to get up off the couch to change TV channels and most of us now effectively use technology. We are on the front-lines of the changes in the world of work: we have parents who had 'good jobs' and some of us might be in the same, fortunate, boat.

Many of us, however, aren't in that same boat and what we were taught about work and how to find and retain it is no longer effective. We're seeking to sort out the changes for ourselves so we can find success, be better role models and actively guide our children towards life/work success.

When I was a young adult in the early-mid '80s, my parents sat me down and explained that theirs was the last generation that could reasonably expect to have one job 'for life' and retire at the end with a pension. I was exceedingly lucky to have parents who not only saw the writing on the wall, but were open to talking about it. My father successfully navigated changes in his work, at times taking lateral positions in the company in order to keep his job. Many weren't so lucky, and found themselves being 'downsized' or 'rightsized' right out of a job. My father's career path was very traditional: he was an engineer employed by a large company. My exposure to the world of work was limited to people who had the status of 'employee'.

One of the most impactful work examples for me was my mother's. My parents were born just prior to World War II and married in 1960. Options for women were limited to 'careers' like teacher, secretary, nurse or nun. It was a time when women to quit school or work when they married. My mother was regularly asked in job interviews whether she planned on having children, because employers weren't keen to employ someone who would leave. The concept of family-friendly workplaces didn't really exist.

My mom stayed at home with us until we were in middle school. Ours was the house that fed lunch to some of the neighbourhood kids whose mothers were at work. When my brother and I hit middle school, my mom took some classes at the local community college and found a job as a receptionist-bookkeeper.

She hated it!

For years she hated it. She called her office 'the piggery'.

In the work I do now, I have created a 'creed for career success' that states:

We are human beings, not human resources. We have the right, the responsibility and the power to find or create work we love. When we contribute from our strengths and values, we benefit ourselves, our families and our communities.

When I talk about finding 'work you love', I don't mean to follow your bliss and leave your brain parked at home. I mean *please* find work that gives you a sense of satisfaction. Work that recognizes and uses your talents. Know who you are and what work will fulfill you so you don't wind up stuck at a piggery.

At the end of the day, the most overwhelming key to a child's success is the positive involvement of parents. ~ Jane D. Hull

My parents' examples were the lessons I most remember when it comes to career guidance. Perhaps we had more formal career education in high school and university, but I certainly don't remember. What I do remember about career education in high school is limited to choosing classes and being advised to 'keep your options open' by staying in math and science. I chose science as my initial career direction because I had good marks and people told me that's where the good jobs were. Plus, going to University was expected and, frankly, I saw it as a way to buy myself 4 more years before having to make any decisions and actually go out and look after myself. This was 1984.

My university career guidance was limited as well, although I accessed more help than some of my peers. My parents arranged for me to take traditional career and personality inventory testing to help me find direction. While it had the potential to help, the assessment results were limited to a long computer printout of job ideas (most of which I didn't understand) and there was no follow up that I recall. We had no career exploration or advice. I longed to be in a Co-Operative education program that had work semesters integrated into our school year, but my marks were too low in university and Co-op was only for 'the smart kids'. Fortunately, my undergraduate research projects gave me the experience I needed to land a permanent research job after university.

When I graduated from Education years later (2002), our career preparation was considerably better but only because we had one professor who made it a course requirement that we complete a portfolio and mock interview prior to the job fair. Even then there was little career exploration. Afterall, an Education degree only really qualifies you to teach in a standard classroom - doesn't it?

* * *

As my Mother puts it, I've now 'quit a number of perfectly good jobs' having worked for 2 biotech companies before retooling as a high school teacher. Eight years ago I took a 1 year leave from high school teaching to help my husband build a business and now find myself self-employed. Eight years later, I've worked sufficiently through the paradigm shifts required to morph from being an employee to being self-employed. In the 'new economy', a change in thinking is really what's required.

The Situation We Find Ourselves In

Obviously (parents) are dealing with a new set of career challenges and they know that they're their children's teachers so it makes them very uneasy these days to think, 'Oh, gee, I'm not getting this career thing right. I don't have the stability or the security and I want my child to feel protected and safe and confident. If I can't do it how am I supposed to teach my child to do it?' ~JT O'Donnell

When my parents sat me down to explain that theirs was the last generation to expect to have one job for life, they gave me great advice. But they couldn't give me the road map because it didn't exist.

Those of us in my generation are the ones making the road map. We're the ones struggling to come to terms with the changes in the economy and the world of work. And we're the ones who can now see that the best reasons to get this thing figured out – regardless of the fears we have to face – are our kids.

A lot of what we were taught about work isn't just outdated, it's now ineffective. And often it's just plain detrimental.

I've heard it said that the longest distance in the world is between our heads and our hearts. We know intellectually that the world of work has changed drastically, but denial is a powerful force. Acknowledging and managing rapid and massive change on the scale we've seen over the past 5-10 years can be frightening and difficult. We've been required to change our attitudes and behaviors significantly from what many of us grew up being taught to think and do.

In any time of massive change, it's important to remember 2 things:

1. There are always fundamental things that won't change, and

2. Change brings opportunities.

Know that the radical shifts we're facing in the economy and the world of work aren't all bad.

* * *

Traditional Job Security Is A Myth

There are 3 outcomes for you in any job: you'll be fired, quit or get laid off. You WILL change jobs. ~Joshua Waldman

I started all of my interviews with a question around job security.

Why?

Because the radical change in what job security means today is at the foundation of the changes we're seeing. Understanding the implications of the change in meaning of these two little words can help up move forward positively and effectively – and help us better navigate our way towards life/work success in a world very different from the one most of us grew up in.

There's no doubt in the minds of the career experts I spoke with that 'job security' means something completely different in the 21st century than it did even in the late 20th century.

Here's what Alexandra Levit had to say about 'job security' in today's world:

Job security means the ability to go to an organization and, expect that you'll be there tomorrow. It doesn't mean that you're going to be there for the next 30 years; that's the attitude of the traditionalist.

People expect something to be fairly predictable where at least if something is coming down the pipe they have some notice of that, and they're able to prepare accordingly.

If the idea that the traditional definition of 'job security' is a myth scares you, rest-assured that you're not alone. The traditional idea of 'job security' is a hard one to shake, because it's comforting to believe the old story that a company will look after you. Many of us grew up with the traditionalist idea of job security and a lot of us were actively discouraged from striking out on our own. We were steered towards the security of finding one long-term job with benefits and a pension.

Things have changed.

The difficulty most of us have today with the changing definition of job security is in fully understanding that when we see the 'something coming down the pipe' we acknowledge it and prepare accordingly. In no small part, the information in this book is here to help you better understand that there are ways to prepare accordingly – so you don't need to fear that which is coming down the pipe to the extent that you ignore it.

Joshua Waldman told me about losing 2 new jobs before he was able to fully understand that 'job security' is a myth. Kelly Green spoke about being laid off after 15 years in an industry. We all have personal stories where either we or people close to us were fired, laid off or quit.

I thought I was going to be in that industry forever, for the rest of my life but, you know, things work out the way they work out and you have to roll with it. ...I know that there are so many people in the same situation. (Kelly Green)

While it's true that job security no longer means having one job for life and retiring with a company pension, people still expect to have some notice of changes in the workplace (Alexandra Levit). The issue that we struggle with in this new definition of job security is that the responsibility to spot future changes in our workplaces now lies with us.

How do we cope in a world where the idea of 'job security' has changed so much that we should now just expect the 'unexpected job loss'?

Job Security Today Comes From You

Job security these days doesn't come from an employer, it comes from yourself. ~Anita Bruzzese

Anita Bruzzese has been writing a syndicated career-related column for 25 years, and like all of us has been experiencing the changes in the world of work first-hand. She's watched things change over the years and observes that people are just now starting to realize the implications of the change in the meaning of 'job security'.

Like others who work in the area of careers, Anita speaks of the lessons we've learned as a result of the recent recession:

You have to be up on your skills. You have to be ready to read that signs that maybe you need to look for another job or another industry which means you need to be up on industry trends. These are all things that a lot of people handed over to their employer (in the past)... You can no longer do that... It really is up to you... People want to help you to a certain degree, but nobody cares about you and your career the way you do.

The employer is no longer responsible for your career.

I don't think it's a coincidence that the recent recession has made people more aware. It's been an emotionally-charged wake-up call. Until we experience a significant emotional event, it can be all-too-easy to ignore the signs and hope that the trouble will just blow over. We're learning first-hand from the recent recession the lesson that my parents tried to teach me when they sat me down to explain how the world of work was changing. My parents were lucky, because while they did see the changes that were coming, my father was able to retire with a pension.

Anita shared her own story of transitioning out of journalism and towards the online world - and more importantly she shared with me the significant emotional event she witnessed years before that made her realize that if the trouble in her field didn't blow over, she absolutely needed a 'Plan B':

> *My own father worked for a company for 30 years and 10 months from retirement the company shut down, laid everybody off and he lost everything. I had been working for a year or so when that happened and that drove home to me that I had to be responsible for Anita and that is a lesson that a lot of people chose to ignore. There was a lot of writing on the wall. There was a lot of talk of this but a lot of people chose to ignore it. They chose instead to go to work every day and believe that if they worked hard enough for this company, the company would take care of them and unfortunately, it does not work out that way for a variety of reasons.*

Anita is not alone in speaking about the absolute necessity of having a 'Plan B'. Others that I interviewed actually echoed Anita's use of the term 'Plan B' – and the increasing necessity that we all have one.

> *Always (have) a 'Plan B'; always (know) what your next move is going to be. Even if you end staying in your career for the next 30 years, you should always have a 'Plan B'. Don't just rely on that one source of income or that one industry and focus on that and put all of your eggs in one basket.*

> *That's one of the things that I've learned myself, and I wasn't even happy at my job. I stayed there just because I thought it was job security but what I really should have been doing at the time was exploring my options and seeing what else was out there and seeing what else was of interest to me. So, that's the one thing I can really say*

about job security. Don't feel like just because you have a job that you're secure in it. (Kelly Green)

Having a 'Plan B' is easy to understand in theory, but very difficult to put into practice. For instance, what **exactly** does 'exploring your options' look like? What activities do you carry out during a typical day when you're 'exploring your options'?

It's easy to look back after-the-fact and realize that we 'should' have noticed the coming change, but we all hold on tightly to hope (or denial) unless something forces us to move ahead, and we have some inkling of what the first steps might look like. Changes in our work life will be easier to navigate when we have some experience with recognizing and creating opportunities, but resilience doesn't guarantee the sailing will be smooth.

Here's Anita's personal experience:

I understand the pain of losing a job. I've watched my parents go through that. I've lost jobs.

...After a while, to keep trying the same thing you're trying just does not make sense. There's so much information out there now and there's so many alternatives. I will be the first to say that when journalism started to change I wasn't sure what I was going to do. My industry wasn't sure what it was going to do. But I got online and I started reading and I started learning and I started reaching out to people, interacting with them saying: How do I start a blog? What is a blog?

I went to blogger conferences. I started interacting on the social networks. I started writing more. I wasn't exactly sure what I was doing but I knew I could see some of that writing on the wall. I couldn't understand completely what it was but I was at least trying something. ...And that paid off for me in a big way when all the full-time journalists in newspaper, and magazines lost their jobs and they needed people to write online.

I had networked like crazy with tons of new people. I reached out every day to somebody new and that helped lead to recommendations for me to get jobs. Did I know exactly what I was doing? No, I didn't. And, was I scared and upset and frustrated? Yes, I was. But at least I felt like I was doing something and that I was moving forward. I wasn't just spinning my wheels.

So when I write about this, I know what people are going through. I've been there; I know exactly what it feels like.

It's important to realize that success isn't always comfortable. Anita had a choice – to remain uncomfortable and fearful and do nothing, or to be uncomfortable and fearful and do something. By far, the advice I heard over and over again from the experts I interviewed was that doing something – anything – was the way towards success. When you're doing something, even if it's not working you have something to assess so you can make changes, try again and move forward. To paraphrase Thomas Edison, you haven't failed, you've merely discovered a number of ways that don't work – and that puts you closer to the solution.

When Anita began her career in journalism, blogging hadn't been 'invented' yet. And this is another consideration when it comes to helping guide our youth towards life/work success. Joshua Waldman observed during our interview that many of the jobs of the future are jobs that haven't been invented yet.

And Dr. Anne Davies devotes her work to supporting educational change that looks forward, not back:

We must prepare all learners for their future, not our past.

Future-proofing our kids for jobs that haven't been invented yet means understanding that job security comes from within each one of us. It comes from being open to the opportunities around us, recognizing them and taking action to move forward rather than holding on to false security of the past.

Job Security Comes From 'Differentiation'

Being open enough to recognize opportunities brings up another aspect of what job security means today.

A number of people spoke about 'differentiation' or 'personal branding' when it comes to job security. You absolutely need to know what makes you stand out. We all need to know what strengths, skills and characteristics we're bringing to a work situation.

> *People think they have a secure job right up until they get fired after being there for 20 years. Real job security is knowing who you are and knowing what you're good at and helping the world in a meaningful way with that, in a way that builds your personal brand so people come to recognize you as the person who has that value. If you do that, you will always have work, in some way or another. ~Scott Dinsmore*

Differentiation, or 'personal branding' is a process to get you started on your way to having a 'Plan B'. The advice the experts outlined during the interviews often centered around aspects of this idea. It's imperative that we help our youth define these things for themselves during school so that the transition from school to work goes more smoothly.

> *When you graduate, you are essentially a clone of the other several hundred thousand people that are also graduating in the same year and time as you. What are you going to do stand out? How are you going to differentiate yourself? ... Don't graduate clueless. ~Lauren Friese*

I'm glad people brought up the concept of Personal Branding because this is the process I use to help people 'find or create work they love'. It's a process of empowerment that helps you first determine what your strengths, skills and values are and then look outward to your communities to see how you can use your strengths to help others.

Knowing how you stand out is empowering as well as pragmatic: when your application is somewhere in a pile of 300, standing out is imperative. Knowing ourselves and what we're great at isn't about falsely propping up our self-esteem – it's about both building confidence and a competitive advantage.

What the 'World of Work' Looks Like Today

May you live in interesting times. ~ Proverb (or Curse!)

In the traditional world of 'job security', we had one job for the long-term. It was a stigma to have a string of jobs.

In today's world, the average length of time people hold a job is 3 years, and it's even shorter for youth (Joshua Waldman and Alexandra Levit).

That's a considerable difference from the 30 years my father worked at one company before retiring with a pension.

Let's think about this a minute. Stigmas die hard. People who haven't been in the workforce for the last 5-10 years, and those who haven't kept current often hold on to old ways of thinking – and the shame and judgements that go with them.

The fear of being stigmatized and judged is very real and it interferes with carrying out an effective job hunt. This is a critical understanding to have when effectively guiding our youth. Consider this story from Anita Bruzzese:

> *At the beginning of the recession it was really hard because people almost seemed ashamed that they had lost their job. I think a lot of them went through (shame) and ...depression and they kept it a secret. They didn't tell people they were looking for work. They didn't tell their neighbor. They didn't tell their cousin. I don't know how many stories I heard where somebody would say, 'I've been looking for work for months. I was sitting at dinner with some friends and somebody's cousin was there and I happened to mention, for the first time, that I was looking*

for work. And sure enough, he connected me with so and so.'

A successful job search depends on letting everyone know you're looking for work – and what that type of work is. When shame keeps you from connecting, it becomes almost impossible to find career success.

Not only did people not change jobs as much in the past, but finding work opportunities was often considerably easier. The judgement that those looking for work face often comes in questions from others that imply that they're lazy or just not looking.

If you've conducted a job search in the recent past, you can attest to the decrease in long-term or full-time job postings. There's been a shift to part-time or contract work. It's not uncommon for employers to use part-time work as a way to screen employees, or to use contract workers for part-time or full-time non-permanent work.

> *I think you see a lot of young people now who, they're doing multiple jobs. To them, it's the most natural thing in the world, to constantly shift and transition. But for older workers it is especially difficult. I had one man say to me, 'You know the last time I looked for a job, I picked up a copy of the New York Times and I circled jobs that I was qualified for.' He said, 'I picked up a copy of the New York Times and there were no jobs in there except for a dishwasher.' He was a very highly skilled professional. He was just floored. He had no clue what was going on because he had not kept up at all. (Anita Bruzzese)*

The changes we're seeing in the definition of 'job security' have significant impact. As we find ourselves having to source 'hard-to-find' work opportunities many times over the course of our lives, our attitudes and actions need to change.

They need to change so we can be more successful in sourcing work for ourselves.

They need to change so we can be more credible and effective role models for our children.

Imagine the older professional from the above example dispensing career advice prior to his enlightenment! Unhelpful career advice from educators, friends and family is one of the biggest frustrations faced by the job hunters and youth I speak with. It's often well-meaning, but that doesn't make it helpful. If you haven't heard 'kids today' being disparaged for a whole host of failings when it comes to the world of work and their ineffective job hunting techniques and ethos, you're in the minority.

Learning how to keep up with currently effective job hunting skills is now a life skill. If you're no longer 'with it', it's very apparent to the people around you who have kept up. Fortunately, keeping up isn't as difficult today as it might have been in the past. Keeping up is as easy as subscribing to a few blogs (and then reading them!). You can access a number of them on Facebook by 'liking' a company's page. Start by getting connected online with the experts I interviewed for this book.

Life/Work Integration & Other Changes

Remember the flight of an airplane. When an airplane takes off it has a flight plan. However, during the course of the flight, wind, rain, turbulence, air traffic, human error, and other factors keep knocking the plane off course. In fact, a plane is off course about 90 percent of the time. The key is that the pilots keep making small course corrections by reading their instruments and talking to the control tower. As a result, a plane reaches its destination.
~ Sean Covey (The 7 Habits of Highly Effective Teens)

One of the 'A-ha' moments I had when speaking with Alexandra Levit was that she introduced me to the concept of 'life/work integration' rather than the concept of life/work balance. Many of us have struggled with the changing expectations in the world of work and have found life/work balance to be elusive.

It's because, like Covey's airplane example, we rarely achieve balance for long. We need to remember that 'balance' requires ongoing input - it's a process not a goal. The idea of life/work integration better reflects the ongoing effort required.

Alexandra Levit, had other insight into how the world of work has changed, and how it might continue to change. As we move away from an industrial economy and further into a global knowledge economy, we're going to be required to be available outside of the traditional 9-5 schedule of a factory.

It's easy to see why it's more important than ever to know who we are and what skills we have to offer. Why it's important to focus on developing personal leadership skills and to know how to deal with what is now being called 'life/work integration' as we move into the future:

There's an emphasis on virtual teaming and being able to collaborate with people across cultures, across seas, across time zones - recognizing that there is no such thing as a 9 to 5 workday anymore. You could be taking a conference call at 10 o'clock at night if it's 7 o'clock in the morning for somebody else and you just have to be willing to roll with the punches.

We (will) also see in the next 5 to 10 years or so, the rise of the continued workforce. Meaning, one person is not going to work for one organization. You will be in a position of doing project work for a variety of different organizations and that's going to happen as organizations start to outsource more things that aren't their core area of expertise. They'll maintain smaller workforces, companies will be less hierarchical and you'll come into your specific function and move on.

We've got a lot of work to do to prepare the American workforce for that change. We are not quite there yet.

Alexandra isn't alone in making this prediction. Some of us are already working in this way or at least moving in this direction.

I had a full-time local contract while I was starting this book project and was able to schedule many of the interviews between 6 -8 am. I live on the west coast – and took full advantage of the 2-3 hour time difference to interview people on the east coast. I found a virtual assistant online who could transcribe the interviews and she was able to provide written transcripts digitally via the internet. This process relied heavily on technologies that weren't available even 10 years ago.

Is this good? Technology certainly allowed me to connect with people I would never have even known about before the Internet. Technology allowed me to quickly outsource the transcription work. That was powerful. For a few weeks, though, I was working very long days. That's a decision I made about short-term life/work integration. This is just the tip of the iceberg. Think about how technology has crept into your own life over the last decade, and the impact it's had on our expectations of response time either from ourselves or others.

> The first challenge we have is that work has been coming home with us thanks to lovely little tools! We feel compelled to have them attached to us so we're not shutting work off when we leave. We've become so accessible that we can't shut off.
>
> We've blurred the lines of what is acceptable in terms of connecting with our coworkers, with our managers, etc. I definitely think that's created a new level of stress for some people.
>
> ...The rate at which we're using all these technologies is overwhelming. A great example is email. Imagine how many emails people got 15 years ago on a daily basis at work versus today. How do you process that? ~ JT O'Donnell

We're increasingly being expected to be available 24/7, yet how many of us have renegotiated the terms of our employment? Are you still expected to be 'seen' at your workplace during traditional hours as well as being on-call? Do you have flexibility in your office hours as a result?

Are you really expected to be on-call? Whose expectation is this? Were you asked or have you offered because you feel you're 'supposed to'? How has that affected your stress and anxiety levels? Your family time?

How has that affected your attitude towards your employer or your employment situation? Do you proactively address these issues, or step back and blame the situation? The economy? Your employer?

We have a whole new way to work, and yet we're often hesitant to set boundaries or negotiate more acceptable terms for our work because in the past, the employer-employee relationship wasn't as equal as it's now becoming. The idea of having personal power and questioning the relationship didn't enter most of our minds in the past. Our employer gave us steady employment in exchange for (often unquestioning) loyalty.

Navigating this change positively requires us to fully take responsibility for our work lives, and to embrace our personal power.

Learning how to take on our personal power can be difficult. And that's an understatement. This is in no small part what I spoke of when I said it's taken me the last 5 years to better understand what it means to shift from an employee mindset to thinking of myself as a business owner.

We're All 'A Business Of One'

So, for parents, what I want them to understand is that your children won't work for anybody anymore. They need to firmly believe they work with them and that with this every job is temporary, that they are a business of one and they have to understand and get comfortable with the concepts of running their own business. (JT O'Donnell)

It's such a domino effect! On the surface, the changes in the economy had an impact on job security – on the number of full-time permanent jobs that had become the norm and the expectation.

But the implications go much deeper. As we find ourselves shifting our attitudes and strategies to source the 80%+ of jobs that aren't posted and aren't permanent – we find we have to get better connected to our communities and networks, get crystal clear on our strengths and how they fit with the needs of potential employers or clients.

It requires us to understand that empowering ourselves to run our 'Business of One' requires changing some long-held and very deep patterns of thinking. When we realize that we really are a 'Business of One' we take on responsibility for ourselves and our work life. The attitude shift from working for an employer, to working with an employer is fundamental and life-altering.

Remember what Alexandra Levit said about virtual teaming and working across time zones; that work in the future will happen more as 'outsourcing' as we contribute not just to one, but to many companies with our skills.

> *What we all have to learn is that... every day you have to go to work with the mindset (that) your employer is basically your client. What are you doing for that client today to make money and what are you doing to secure your own future? If you think that you can sit back and do the job every day and that will get you your reward, it doesn't work that way anymore and you have to take responsibility for that. (Anita Bruzzese)*

One of the biggest challenges for many parents in helping their children create career success will be in understanding what is required in today's world of work and not letting their past difficulties and frustrations color their advice:

> *I feel like we're at the lowest point of the relationship between employee and employer... We had a time where they helped each other, they trusted each other and we've started to see it disintegrate... which is one of the reasons*

I think that the dissatisfaction rate is so high. A lot of people recognize they have golden handcuffs and they struggle with that. They're angry.

...I just hope (parents) don't continue to push that on to the younger generation because it's going to be a lot harder for that generation to work with employers if they're that angry at such a young age. I hear this all the time from young people. 'My parents told me how awful it was and don't do this...'

I had a 20-something tell a manager that he would not stay after 5 o'clock. They had a big project and (the manager) asked everybody to stay after 5 o'clock to get this project done.

(The 20-something) went off and took a phone call and came back and said, 'I just talked to my parents and I'm not staying.'

The manager asked, 'What did you say?'

'Look, my parents made it clear to me the moment I start working overtime hours for you, you'll be asking for it all the time and I'll be sucked in and working crazy hours and you won't pay me any more for it and I'm not doing it. I need to set my boundaries now.'

I think, what a career limiting move for this young person...Per the advice of the parents. I just hope that we don't project that. I want our young people to learn how to be 'Businesses of One', but I don't want them to be doing it because they hate the very companies that they're going to partner with. (JT O'Donnell)

This is a wonderful illustration of the idea of taking on personal power. We want to empower our kids to create success, not help them limit their careers.

The changes in the workplace happened for many of us 'mid-stream'. The employer-employee contract changed for Boomers and Gen-Xers slowly and at a time when many of us were already 'entrenched' with family obligations. Many of us found ourselves wearing the 'golden handcuffs' because we felt we were too far down the road towards a pension (or in denial or fear) to pack things in and take a risk trying something new.

Our kids are in a different position. The changes in the workplace are permanent. Things will continue to evolve, but we won't return to the 'traditional' 9-5 work day. We won't launch our children into life/work success with 'traditional' ways of thinking or the anger that many of us still feel with employers.

We need to ensure that our children develop their personal power and learn how to positively negotiate for themselves. Like Joshua Waldman found after being laid off from a few jobs in a short space of time, it takes time and effort to do the healing.

Moving forward means being clear on your direction, taking charge of your own career and acting on the attitude that you're working with an employer:

Everyone is busy doing their own thing so you need to be the one who proactively sets goals with your manager and decides where you want to take your career. I think if you get into that mindset now, you'll be well positioned to do that for real when you're not working for one organization any longer. (Alexandra Levit)

Kids These Days!

The children now love luxury; they have bad manners, contempt for authority; they show disrespect for elders and love chatter in place of exercise. Children are now tyrants, not the servants of their households. They no longer rise when elders enter the room. They contradict their parents, chatter before company, gobble up dainties at the table, cross their legs, and tyrannize their teachers.
~ Socrates

Damn kids.

When it comes to helping our youth transition more smoothly from school to the world of work, we adults are still often guilty of stereotyping and disrespecting our youth. Good to know things haven't changed appreciably since a few hundred years BCE.

Youth and young adults are growing up in a very different world than the one we did. The change we see the most easily is the rapid development of technology. Today's youth are what we call 'digital natives' – they don't remember a time before the Internet. Many teens and most young adults have 24/7 Internet access via smart phone. Many don't have their digital non-native parents and teachers in their technological space to offer guidance and supervision.

Think 'Lord Of The Flies'.(My apologies for the high school English class reference. For those of you with no memory of reading LOTF, it's about a group of school boys whose plane crash lands on a deserted island, and their ensuing descent into savagery as they face survival without adult supervision.)

There are other critical forces shaping our youth: they've watched the upheaval in the world and the impact it's had on the adults. They've been shaped during a time of great changes in technology, the environment, globalization, and the economy. The younger millennials don't remember when there wasn't a war. They've watched their parents' and grandparents' generations struggle to keep up with massive changes.

Many have been (over)protected by parents who want to shield them from the massive upheavals and dangers in the world, and who just want their kids to feel 'protected, safe and confident' as JT O'Donnell put it.

We've already seen that youth have trouble finding work (too often attributed to laziness), and when they do find work they don't keep it long (don't forget that most of us aren't keeping jobs long either). According to the experts I interviewed, the average job length for adults is 3 years, the average for youth is about 18 months.

Given all of this, it's easy to understand why generational researcher Bruce Tulgan has observed that those born in the 1990s 'grew up way too fast and never grew up at all.' Millennials are often accused of hiding behind technology, but the accusations are never helpful. We need to better understand what lies behind the behaviour:

> Young people today (have) been able to self-edit through technology. Their biggest fear is saying the wrong thing... This generation hates to disappoint, hates it. They don't want to see if you're upset with them. That's why they hide behind that technology. I had a client tell me in the course of four months, they had two 20-somethings resign by text message. $50,000 a year jobs and they resigned through text message because they don't want to have to see the manager in person.

> And (the manager's) solution was, 'I'll never hire a young person again.' That was the person's comment and you think, 'But you don't understand the other side.' ~JT O'Donnell

This in no small way explains the often-heard story about youth requiring micro-management from employers. They're often considered 'professionally immature' (JT O'Donnell). This attitude is disappointing to me because I can tell you similar stories about 'clueless' coworkers I had when I was a 20-something. We need to be more aware that sometimes the 'failings' we're attributing to youth are failings we had ourselves 'back in the day'. Dr. Woody pointed out that these 'failings' are often a result of our life stage than the result of the generation we belong to.

* * *

Another of the characteristics that youth today are often criticized for is that they have a lack of loyalty to an employer. I've heard this first-hand from Boomer and Gen-X parents right after they tell me their stories of being 'rightsized' and 'downsized' and how they now find themselves struggling to work as a contractor.

Loyalty to an employer is the flip side of job security. In return for job security, we are expected to give loyalty to our employer.

So before we criticize our youth for lacking loyalty, let's take a minute to remember that they've grown up watching us being 'downsized' and 'rightsized' right out of employment, and some of us right out of the pension that we were 'right' to expect when we started working. The rules changed somewhere along the way and the reward for our loyalty is unemployment and no pension.

> *The bigger problem we have right now is that most of us that are parents grew up in a time when you were told: 'You go to work, you stay at that company for a long time, they give you loyalty if you give them loyalty in exchange. But, that just doesn't happen anymore.*
>
> *There's a reason we say every job is temporary - it's not to be mean. I've had some employers get indignant about it and say 'That's not true.' But it is. Why don't we just call it for what it is? You can't guarantee that someone will still be doing the same job at your company a year from now, let alone whether you can keep them. (JT O'Donnell)*

The job searching tactics we needed to find work when we were sourcing it infrequently just aren't effective in a world where we're continually sourcing new work opportunities. Our kids know it because they've been watching and listening. We might think we're giving good advice, but the only ones we're fooling are ourselves. Kids know that 'traditional' job security is a myth even if older adult workers and employers haven't yet acknowledged it.

This isn't the only piece of thinking that's outdated. The old story about staying in school and finding a job at the end of it has changed. Is it any wonder that students today are struggling with engagement in school?

> *Young people struggle with having been misled as high school students to think that if they went to a university they'd have a job at the end of it. That may have been the situation for the people advising them but it is definitely not the situation for today's students and recent graduates. (Lauren Friese)*

When we give advice to kids about following the 'proper' pathway from education to a 'good job' (often defined as long-term permanent work), it just isn't helpful today. And our kids know it. When I spoke with Michael Woodward (Dr. Woody), he made it clear that when there's a disconnect between what parents say and what parents do, children will follow our actions, not our advice.

* * *

Alexandra Levit has worked with the Business Roundtable's Springboard Project, which advised the Obama administration on current workplace issues. She has some great insight on one of the behaviors we often criticize: the use of technology.

> *Basic communication (is) the area where the Millennials fall down a bit. They rely so heavily on social media for communication. I was in an international airport a few years ago and I saw a teen group going overseas together. They were taking a class trip and they were all sitting in those row of chairs at the airport. Every single chair was taken by one of these kids and they were all on*

their devices. It was completely silent, nobody was talking about anything. You know they were texting each other, IM'ing each other back and forth and they weren't actually speaking to each other. It just really crystalized in my mind: Wow, that's something these guys are really missing.

This observation is interesting when we think about JT O'Donnell's idea that this generation fears disappointing someone else or doing the wrong thing. Alexandra's observation reinforces to us the down-stream consequences of their fear of disappointing and lack of communication skills: lack of practice with basic job hunting skills.

How can we expect our kids to perform well in the workplace when they're afraid to make a mistake? Or find it difficult to hold conversations – let alone the difficult ones.

* * *

The picture just gets more bleak for a generation afraid to make mistakes and disappoint people when we consider that in today's world of work, none of us has any idea about all of the opportunities 'out there'. Jobs of the future haven't been invented yet.

One of the issues identified during the interviews was that in today's world of work we're spoiled for choice. There are so many options for us and given our overloaded culture, this can lead to paralysis.

The biggest obstacle is in having too much choice. I talked to my grandmother about this several years ago. I said, 'Grandma, I don't know how you lived when you did where you had no choice, you had to stay home and raise kids.' She (said), 'Actually that was a lot easier than what you're going through. You're able to do anything you want. How paralyzing that is.' I thought about that really carefully and I think that makes a lot of sense. There are so many things that are on the radar that you could

*potentially do that I think people do get paralyzed and they
don't do anything because they're not able to make a
choice. ~Alexandra Levit*

'Kids These Days' face a number of challenges in their
transition from adolescence into adulthood: some resulting
from the fact that they're kids, and some resulting from
growing up in turbulent and changing times. When our
youth are at a critical period in their transition from
adolescence to adulthood, many of us are still struggling to
make sense ourselves of the changes in the world.

As a result, many of our youth find themselves being
guided by adults who have don't have a strong
understanding of the changes taking place, or of the forces
that have had a significant impact on our youth. This is a
combination that leads to frustration and blame.

If our goal truly is to help guide our youth towards life/
work success, it's necessary that we learn to listen to and
understand how their lives are different from our own,
while at the same time helping them to master the skills
they're going to need to move ahead.

Who's job is this? Parents? Educators? Employers?

Proactive employers are realizing that they also have a
responsibility to meet this generation where they are and
provide some workplace training, especially if they hope to
find and retain talented youth.

Educators are often on the receiving end of blame for
'not teaching that' in school. It's no secret that the
educational system is in crisis itself as it tries to cope with
the massive changes. It's easy to say that kids should get
better career guidance at school, but it's best not to hope
that changes will come any time soon.

Like job security, career guidance comes from you! As
we've already seen, some of our most impactful career
lessons come from our parents' example. It's important for

each one of us that we're 'with it' when it comes to understanding the realities of the world of work for ourselves.

Don't forget that a world of up-to-date career information is available to you online by connecting with the experts who contributed to this work... and getting connected is one of the life/work success skills that we all need in order to stay 'with it'.

Career Education Is The Key To Youth Engagement

To bring a child up in the way he should go, travel that way yourself ~ Josh Billings

What was your experience of career education in school?

I outlined my experiences with career education during the 1980s at the beginning of the book. It was rather limited and disjointed. If it wasn't for guidance from my parents, I really don't know whether I'd have had the presence of mind to evolve in my work life.

Their ideas about the myth of job security were almost heretical at the time. I didn't realize how heretical they were until I was in my mid-20s and a friend explained about his life/work plans. They included 'getting on full-time permanent' before getting married and having kids. I think an argument about the myth of job security ensued. I really was fortunate that my parents had read me the memo. His hadn't.

Career Education In School Is Often Irrelevant

Do you remember in high school... I remember sitting in a room and taking this big long test for 2 days. Then I met with the guidance counselor and the counselor sat down and gave me this printed out list of the types of jobs that I qualify for with no descriptions. It is the most random collection of jobs with no explanation... He tossed it. It made no sense. ~JT O'Donnell

Does this sound familiar? Many of the aspects of career education as I experienced them, and as JT O'Donnell remembers are repeated by other people I speak with. Many had even less in the way of career guidance and most stories are those of horrifically bad advice and limited thinking. This isn't limited to people who graduated decades ago – it's a story we're still hearing. Test it out for yourself!

I've recently heard an example of a high school guidance counsellor the students refer to as 'The Dream Killer', and I've spoken with career education coordinators who are frustrated with the current state of career education. Much of the advice our kids are receiving isn't much better than the advice we received decades ago.

Career advice repeats the same misleading story Lauren Friese spoke about earlier: going to college or university is a requirement for getting a 'good' job. Youth often view their career guidance as being just not relevant, and they're often (rightly) distrustful of the advice they're being given.

They're getting old advice, and yet we know times have changed.

It doesn't come as a surprise that the educational institutions are slow to respond. Firstly, that's the nature of institutions – they don't turn on a dime. Secondly, many of us of the age to be giving career advice grew up in a time when there was less need for effective career skills – and our own skills aren't current. Let's not forget that the changes in the world of work are not only recent and massive, but continuous.

The solution isn't to blame the institution, but to realize that parents (and educators) have the power to start making positive change themselves.

Our kids can't wait for institutional change. Parents have the capacity to not only help guide their children towards life/work success, but also to help them engage in their educations in the process.

We have the power.

* * *

In a few of the interviews, I asked people why they thought that youth just aren't accessing career education when advice is readily available.

Despite what we think of as less than adequate career education, we do have access to information and guidance during our high school years, in college or university, and increasingly online. There is no shortage of online career advice available – answers to any career-related question are no further than a Google search away.

I think there are two reasons (for youth not accessing career services). It can either be because they're not ready... or because they don't feel it's' relevant to them.

... That was also something I personally experienced and we see and hear a lot from the students that use Talent Egg. They're thinking, 'finally something for me, finally a resource that doesn't talk down to me or that isn't just for everybody. It's for people exactly like me.' (Lauren Friese)

Relevance was a theme that came up repeatedly. Joshua Waldman spoke about accessing his Alumni career center after he graduated only to find that it wasn't equipped to handle his specific needs.

Career education can't be the 'one-size-fits-all' endeavour that many students experience. In Canada, we've identified that there will be a shortage of workers in the skilled trades. As a result, there are programs focused on recruitment in those areas. Whether we're advising students that they 'must' go to college or university in order to get a job, or look into the skilled trades, they're all-too-aware that traditional career services often have an agenda.

I did visit my career services once. I thought I should. (Between) the testing that I took there and after I spoke to the counselor, they told me that I would probably be a good teacher. I think that that's kind of fallback recommendation of career counselors and also of guidance counselors at the high school level for anybody who doesn't know that they want to work in business and doesn't know that they want to work in engineering. (Lauren Friese)

When I took those tests in university in the late '80s, I too was also given a list of jobs I would be suited for, except 'military service' was close to the top. I suspected a recruitment scheme.

Youth are sensitive to being 'sold' on advice they know is outdated, or is selling someone else's agenda (whether it's a parent or an educational institution). Their reaction is to tune out the advice because they no longer trust the authority. Sadly, they may well be very suited to the area they're being steered towards, but they may never find out if they've disengaged from the advice.

This isn't a criticism of youth. It shows they're perceptive. It's right to question any authority when it's trying to force an agenda. It's annoying when someone tries to sell you on their viewpoint without listening to or trying to understand yours.

The traditional career service and all the things related to it such as info-sessions and career fairs are not necessarily appealing to a new generation that wants things when they want it, where they want, and made exactly tailored to them. (Lauren Friese)

Is this too much to ask? Before you say, 'Yes', remember that adults demand no less. We live in a world where we all expect to be able to access the information we need when we need it.

Making Career Education Relevant

There are 2 main reasons youth don't access career education – because they just aren't ready, and because it isn't relevant – and these issues can both be addressed simultaneously.

Really? Really!

Career Education has a critical role to play in re-engaging youth in school and in their life beyond. But it needs to be relevant – taking into account the real needs of the students at different stages of their life. We must shift our thinking towards empowering and encouraging kids on an ongoing basis, rather than continuing with a top-down agenda to fill seats in colleges, universities and trade schools.

This doesn't mean that our kids won't attend colleges, universities and trade schools. It means that when they go, they'll go because they choose to go, not because they feel they're 'supposed to'.

> *I think that any way you can encourage a young person to engage in their career from an early age... the better.*

> *... And to expect everybody to know what they want at that age is really misguided and wrong. (Lauren Friese)*

Traditional career education focuses on having us ask ourselves, 'What do I want to be when I grow up'? It's not always effective. If you're like me, you know many adults who still struggle with this question! Usually, they laugh as they say they're still trying to figure out what they want to be, but their struggle underscores the ineffectiveness of our basic career education.

Most of us perceive career education and guidance as something to be accessed in school. We've traditionally thought that when school ends, so does our career education. We're now moving away from traditional models of education and towards a belief that education and training happen over the course of our lives. This thinking needs to include career education and guidance as well. Our careers aren't static. They change with our life stage and are affected by outside forces (as we're currently being reminded by the changing economy).

In traditional career education we present students with a limited number of job options, focus on writing resumes and learning how to attend career fairs and stare at job boards. In the traditional way of thinking, it's hard to reconcile how we can engage students at a young age in career education and not stream them towards certain types of work before they're ready to make an informed decision.

How do parents support career education and give effective guidance that's relevant and age-appropriate? Career education that doesn't try to 'sell' our children on a career goal that isn't theirs? Or focuses on a job that won't be there? Or for a job we can't predict will be there?

We need to shift our basic career guidance question. Instead of asking, 'What do you want to be when you grow up', we need to shift our basic career education question to:

WHO are you? ~Rumeet Billan

It's time to shift our basic career guidance question and help our children and youth develop a more solid foundation of self-awareness.

Explore, Explore, Explore!

What is the work you can't not do? ~Scott Dinsmore

Job one in guiding young adults toward career success is to help them truly explore the options that are available to them. This has been the missing piece for many of us, and continues to be the missing piece for many of our youth.

Given the vast number of potential opportunities out there for us in today's world – many of which haven't been invented yet – knowing who we are is a better place to start than trying to figure out what we want to be. While it can take some exploration to get really clear on who we are, there are tools that are commonly used by career developers and educators to help us at least get pointing in the right direction.

There's no area of study required in high school for… becoming a self-expert, (in) understanding your natural strengths and talents. What are you bad at? What do you hate? Based on your past experiences, what do people thank you for? What are the things that you wake up early to do. Then, you can actually define what success means to you. If you don't, you're going to adopt some predefined societal version that doesn't mean anything...

...It (wouldn't) even take that long. You spend like an hour a week while you're in school, it'd be crazy what you'd learn. Or just take the Strengths-Finder 2.0 test; it will take a half hour and you'll be blown away. (Scott Dinsmore)

It's important to realize that understanding who you are isn't solely an internal process. One of the questions Scott asked was 'what do people thank you for'? Sorting out who you are is a social process. It requires developing interpersonal skills along the way. Social skills help us all assess how we are being received. Knowing what we do that people thank us for is an important skill – because the adult version of this question is 'what do people pay you for'?

The sooner we start to help our youth with this personal understanding and exploration, the better because this isn't just about finding your career direction as you near graduation, it's about helping our youth engage in their educations and take what learning they can with them into their futures.

The great news is that it seems that this is already happening! The experts I spoke with who work in the growing area of business coaching and entrepreneurship are beginning to see more engagement and career exploration. Entrepreneurial education helps youth learn about themselves AND find real-world problems that they can solve.

People are exploring different options. They're not necessarily going out for that one job right out of college and thinking that they're going to stay there the rest of their life. ...Young people; are becoming more entrepreneurial. They're actually doing more research and trying different things and (they're) not set on one specific industry and thinking that's going to secure them the rest of their lives. The one biggest change I think I've seen in the last 5 to 10 years is that people are really more open to different options and they're more willing to go out there and step out on a limb. (Kelly Green)

The change in the idea of traditional job security and the difficulty that people – youth in particular – are having finding 'secure' employment may be what's started this movement towards exploration and entrepreneurism.

* * *

Taking advantages of opportunities to put students into workplaces, whether as job shadows or in longer-term situations was thought to be critical by a number of the people interviewed. In Canada, there's a program called, 'Take Our Kids To Work Day' (TOKTWD) that happens every November. Grade 9 students job shadow a parent or other adult. It's a significant amount of work on the part of employers/employees and the teachers who are responsible for doing the prep work and placements, but it is an opportunity for students to get an introduction to a real workplace. When I worked in the biotech industry, our office participated in this program and we made an effort to showcase all of the jobs available at the company and to have the students tour the offices, labs and manufacturing facilities.

> I think the biggest overlooked opportunity in high school is the concept of 'Take Your Kids To Work Day'. The only way to really know what a job is like is to try it. In high school it's really hard to get the opportunity to try and be an accountant or try to be a construction worker because you're 15 or 16 years old. The 'Take Your Kids To Work Day' is a unique opportunity to actually visit a real life job site.

> For me, for example, I thought I wanted to work in film. I went and spent 2 days on a film set and what I learned was there's a lot of waiting around, it's freezing, you're outside all the time, you're carrying heavy equipment. It's a lot of work and it's not what I thought it was. I learned from that not only did I not want to work in film but I also learned that I didn't want to work outside, I didn't want to work in any manual labor at all, and that I had the patience of a 4 year old. So, working in anything where waiting was involved wasn't going to be career. That kind of career learning is not something that you get from reading a book or a piece of software like career cruising, or something like that. Take advantage of any opportunity you have to be exposed to the real life workplace. (Lauren Friese)

The value for youth in experiences like this is increased when parents and educators follow up by helping youth sort out which parts of the experience were interesting and which parts weren't. In any job there will be tasks involved that aren't at the top of anyone's 'favorites' list, but it's important to decide which are things we put up with as 'part of the job', and which are 'deal breakers'. Learning which of these is which is an ongoing process that we all hone with age and experience.

The sooner we start having work-like experiences and reflecting on them, the better!

Informational Interviewing

It does really work, informational interviewing. That's really the big component that we don't give kids enough of. (JT O'Donnell)

One of the most effective tools for both career education and conducting an effective job search is the informational interview. It's also vastly under-used, and many people aren't yet aware of what an informational interview is!

A job interview is set up by a company when they're looking for a new employee. An informational interview is a short interview set up by any person seeking information. The interviewer can be exploring a career area or a specific industry or job. The purpose of the interview is NOT to ask for a job, but to ask questions about the interviewee's experiences in their industry and to seek advice. Informational interviews are great tools for expanding your networks.

Usually informational interviews are short – on the order of 15-20 minutes. They consist of about 5 questions prepared ahead of time, and so aren't difficult to carry out. The benefits to these short conversations are enormous. The career explorer starts to find out important pieces of information that can help guide them in their career decision-making process, and they begin to expand their personal and/or professional networks.

If your young person hasn't yet been exposed to informational interviewing, this is certainly something that you can help them set up. As with any effective career skill, it's important that our youth see us modeling these skills. They're invaluable for all of us.

Informational interviewing is also an effective tool because it helps youth answer their own career exploration questions.

Find more information about informational interviewing on my website: CampbellDuke.com/informational-interviews.

* * *

When we ask the traditional 'what do you want to be when you grow up' question, it implies that we will each have one job that we're locked into for life. It precludes the idea of career exploration because once you've found the one thing you're 'supposed' to be doing you stop looking. We can use the new career question ('who are you') to help youth explore career options while they're finding their way in the world of work.

> *So, what I tell high school students and college students (is to) make an intelligent first step. Go into a job. Don't worry about finding your life's passion because that may or may not happen; passion is not all it's cracked up to be. Go into a job that will allow you to acquire as many transferable skills as possible. Transferable skills are skills that are relevant across the wide variety of industries and roles; things like project management, sales, client relations, marketing, finance. Therefore, if you're able to learn some of those then you can really take those anywhere you want to go. Almost any job offers opportunities for transferable skills. Even working at McDonald's, if you think about that – high management, client relations. These are things based all about the way you view a job not necessarily the job itself. Stop putting so much pressure to find that perfect thing because that's going to result in a lot of disappointment. (Alexandra Levit)*

Finding our life's 'passion' is a process, and it is developed and honed by what we learn from the work we do – including what we get out of our first jobs.

If we want to move towards our 'perfect job', we need to become aware of what we're learning from the first jobs we have.

For example, when my step sons were first thinking about finding jobs while they were in high school, we talked about what jobs they might apply for. The oldest was looking to find anything, preferably something that paid above minimum wage, because he was interested in making money to support a car and his social life. He's extroverted and good at understanding processes, so finding a position in retail was relatively easy. We talked to both boys about exactly what Alexandra Levit spoke about: that every job is necessary for the functioning of the business or the employer wouldn't be hiring you. There is something to learn from every job you have. You learn about yourself – what you like, what you don't like, what people thank you for... You learn about the business – what do you like about how its run, why is it run the way it's run...

This advice doesn't just hold for jobs – it also applies to any work or volunteer experience.

For all of us, the key is in learning to reflect on our experience and take action on this growing awareness. Learning to see the value in the work we're doing is a critical life/work success skill.

Questioning is what we do best when we're young! Use this to explore and discover answers for yourself. Make the most of opportunities – and failures! Informational interviewing is one of the most valuable life/work success tools. The earlier we learn how to connect with someone who can answer our questions, the more successful we will be.

Be Clear on Values: Know Why

Your values are what guide you in making decisions in uncertain times or in novel circumstances. ~Dr. Michael 'Woody' Woodward

We're certainly living in a time of uncertainty and novel circumstances! And we've heard a number of examples from those interviewed about the struggles many of us are having in finding life/work success and satisfaction in a fast-changing world of work because much of what we've learned about what successful decisions and job hunting behaviors look like have changed. Dr. Woody works with professionals and entrepreneurs and he shared what he sees as a fundamental aspect of people who are successful:

Those who are successful will talk about the values that they've learned throughout their life journey.

When speaking to parents, I would say identify and articulate a core set of values... that will help your children understand how to make (the) good decisions that will help them get to where they want to go.

(Parents) have to know their own values because you can't help guide your children if you don't even have the sense, or direction, yourself. You have to look at your own personal ethic and what kind of things have been successful (for you) or that you've seen (in) others around you who are successful. How do you role model those behaviors and those values? How do you expose your kids to positive role models or people who have a success-oriented mentality? How do you make sure they see it, that they get it?

You (have to) wrap the bow around it by articulating it and putting it into simple words or simple terms that (your children) can understand and they can remember, and they can fall back on. Parents aren't always going to be there for every decision a kid has to make. So, they've got make sure that they clearly instill in them what to fall back on in a situation where they don't know what the answer is, (when) they don't know what choice to make.

So, instead of relying on facts or knowledge, which they may not have, what is their instinct telling them?

That instinct should come from a core set of guiding principles that their parents have helped them articulate and understand.

Very few people find it easy to answer the question, 'Why are you doing what you're doing', whether they're talking about work or life. Articulating our values can take some discussion. Scott Dinsmore spoke about the work transition he made after finding 'a proper job' he wasn't suited for, and then he found people coming to him for advice:

...Along the way, people started to ask for help. It wasn't like I was doing anything special, I was just asking one simple question: 'Why are you doing what you're doing?' They'd look at me and think for a second and say, 'Well, because I'm supposed to, right?' And, you could see the look on their faces. As soon as they said that out loud, they noticed that was a really bad answer. ...We start asking 'why' enough times, (and we) get to the foundation of something.

One of Dr. Woody's pieces of advice was to 'attack the premise of any question'. Asking 'why' we're saying or doing something is one way to help us get to the foundation of a problem, but also to help us really understand what values are important to us.

We often pay lip-service to a value that we don't really 'live' because it's a social expectation:

There's a difference between an aspirational value or a value that you cling to but don't believe versus the value that you live in everyday life. Often times, people will look at (a value) and say, well, this value seems important or seems socially desirable so that's my value even though I don't do anything to actually live it.

When it comes to parents instilling values, (parents) have to understand what their own values are. They have to clearly articulate what they are, and they have to think about: 'How do I live and role model these values in a very deliberate way that my children can see? They can also see me not just doing but they can also see the benefit of it.'

Kids are very perceptive... They see more than they hear. They pay more attention to what you do. So, if what you're doing is incongruent with what you say, you send a mixed message and kids will fall back on what you do.

Kids *are* very perceptive. They ask questions, and we all challenge authority (or at least complain about it) when we see a disconnect between what is being said and what is being done. Dr. Woody observed that the successful entrepreneurs (of all ages) he works with are skilled at reflecting on the gap between an aspirational value and the values they actually live. They've had experience in asking the questions and being very realistic about what they're doing. Parents can help create their own success and set kids up for success by asking themselves questions about their own values:

What are our values? What's important to us? What do we want our kids to see? How do we want them to act and behave and what can we do very deliberately to instill that? This is what I see in successful entrepreneurs: They're very able to look inward, to be thoughtful, to be reflective, to be introspective, and then figure out 'How do I take that and project that forward or outwardly in a very positive, fruitful way? How do I go with where my strengths are?'

Being clear about our lived values is important for our own life/work success, and helping our kids identify and articulate their values will help them navigate 'uncertain times and novel circumstances'. But there's more to life/work success... and being clear about our natural inclinations is another big piece of the life/work success picture.

Understand Your Skills

Hide not your talents. They for use were made. What's a sundial in the shade? ~ Benjamin Franklin

With all of the recent changes to the world of work, I asked Dick Bolles about 'traditional' workplace and job hunting skills that HAVEN'T changed over the 40 years he's been writing 'What Color Is Your Parachute'.

The great news is that while job hunting practices might look superficially different in today's job market than they did when we were job hunting, the fundamentals are the same.

Job hunters are looking to match their skills with the skills required by an employer (or potential client). We're still looking for a place where we can contribute and be effective.

One of the issues with the use of the word 'skill' is that it's often has different meanings to different groups of people.

Employers, for example, talk about "he didn't have the necessary skills," when what they really mean is "he didn't have four plus years in the food industry, marketing to 20-28 year olds." In other words they really mean "experience."

Job-hunters on the other hand often talk about skills as "can fix computers" or "being good with people." They really mean "results." (Dick Bolles)

It's important that we all understand what employers mean when they ask for 'skills' and want to know about experience.

Mr. Bolles referred to the work of Sidney Fine, who wrote 'The Dictionary of Occupational Titles', and who was also responsible for the definitions of job-related skills that are in use today. Understanding the differences in what the different categories of 'skills' are can help all of us to better put words to our wide range of skills.

There are 3 main categories of 'Skills':

* **Functional (aka Transferable) Skills:** These skills are often divided into 3 subcategories: Functional and transferrable skills define how you handle people, information or things. The skills in each subcategory range from basic to highly advanced. The more developed your skills are, the more self-directed you are. For instance, in the 'People' category, skills range from 'Able to take instruction' through to 'Able to mentor others'. Someone requiring a lot of direction will need to gain experience and develop leadership abilities as they move towards being able to mentor others.

* **Special-Knowledge Skills:** These are skills that we learn through experience – whether in school or through other specialized training. No matter how skilled we are with interpersonal communications, we just can't be a brain surgeon or a red-seal plumber without gaining special-knowledge skills.

* **Personal-Management Skills:** These are often also called 'traits' and describe aspects of our personality and preferences. Examples of traits would include things like being calm or energetic, patient, cautious...etc.

When we think about guiding our youth towards life/work success, it's helpful to keep these skill categories in mind. Success in finding and retaining work, like creating success in our life is in no small part a function of the combination of the skills we have.

What's more important to understand is that everybody has skills, and skill preferences. Having skills in one area rather than another isn't 'right' or 'wrong'. This isn't like passing at test at school.

What we all need to know is that we have skills, it's how we use them that counts. A question you can ask of yourself and your young adult is: do you prefer working with information, people or things?

Start the discussion on skills by asking your young adult about a favorite activity and what about the activity he or she finds the most interesting. Is it people, information or things? You might be surprised to find out where this leads you!

Your Head or Your Heart?: The Heated Agreement

A vision without a plan is a dream. A plan without a vision is drudgery. But a vision with a plan will change the world.
~ Proverb

We live in a world governed by competition. Win or lose? Up or down? Black or white? Follow your head or follow your heart?

When you start getting more information about career education and guidance, you'll discover that there's often a 'debate' about whether it's best to follow your head or your heart.

We often over-simplify choices as one or the other. When we argue 'head or heart' we do ourselves and our children a great disservice because we're having what I've heard called a 'Heated Agreement'. It's important that we bring both our heads and our hearts to the exploration of careers.

It is possible to follow our hearts and have our brains engaged. I'd argue that it's necessary.

The sooner youth start becoming aware of their unique combination of personality type, interests, strengths, skills and values – and use them to thoroughly explore career options, the more likely they are to become engaged in (and excited about) their educations, work and life. This can only lead to success.

Scott Dinsmore had the opportunity to live in Spain shortly after graduating from school, and seeing another culture's values left a lasting impression on him:

I got to see that people prioritize happiness over other things that most people in the US seem to think are really important like status and money. So I got this new view of the world... but when I got back to the US I still listened to my older mentors that said, 'Get a job with a big

*company'... and I did. After just two weeks, ...I was
slamming my head against the keyboard; it was so
useless for both sides. I was not able to last. 7 months
was my final day...*

*I was so frustrated and I wanted to have some impact on
something... So I went on this discovery path trying to
figure out what went wrong.*

*...I had career coaches and made some discoveries about
myself and what I care about.*

This kind of work we do in a knowledge-based economy
has different demands than work done in an industrial
economy. We don't work 9-5 anymore, so there is far less
separation between work life and home life. This is why we
are moving towards speaking of life/work integration
rather than life/work balance. It's why we hear more about
the importance of integrating your heart in your career
exploration.

I say we have the right, the responsibility and the
power to find work we LOVE. It's a responsibility because
we're now bringing all of who we are to work. Like Scott
Dinsmore experienced, if your work is out of alignment
with your skills, values and world view, you're unhappy
and unproductive. We have a responsibility to ourselves to
be in a work situation that gives us satisfaction so we're
happy. We owe it to our employer so that we're productive.
We owe it to our family so that our time with them is
happier, and we owe it to our communities to be
contributing the best of ourselves.

Rumeet Billan is similarly focused on both her head
and heart in her work contributions. Like Scott, she speaks
about having an impact. Among her many roles, Rumeet is
currently teaching a new Social Entrepreneurship program
at Ontario's Humber College.

*What I'm finding is that a lot of individuals... want to make
a difference. They're thinking, how do I (a) pay the bills,
but also (b) make a social impact? That's where social*

entrepreneurship comes about. It's not only the profit side but it's the impact side.

When parents or teachers or educators are talking, it needs to be clear that you don't need to decide between either or. You can have both.

I would go so far as to say that it's not just possible to have both, success requires that you have both.

This is why shifting out of the 'either/or' mentality is crucial when we're helping guide your youth towards ways of thinking that will serve them well regardless of the state of the economy or our ability to predict what jobs might be out there in the future.

* * *

This desire to make an impact – to think about your values and to contribute something of value from the heart - is more than just the idealism of youth. It's a natural outcome of our shift towards the 'knowledge-based economy'.

I like to tell people I'm a 'high school teacher dropout'. When I last taught in a Canadian high school classroom in 2008, I was working in what was called the 'Career and Academic Readiness Program' at an alternative high school. We were tasked with helping at-risk youth make the transition from middle school to high school – by helping students identify and build on their strengths and skills.

The focus was on building not just self-esteem, but on building internal (intrinsic) motivation. We knew that success skills are the same whether we're talking about success in school, work or life. The goal was to start to build skills that would help students learn how to motivate themselves.

Intrinsic motivation is internal – it's the kind of motivation that comes from your heart. It makes you do what you do. Intrinsic motivation drives you through the tough times. It drives you to keep at a task even when it might seem to yourself and others like you're crazy. Intrinsic motivation helps you make wise decisions and follow through on your own. We contrast this to extrinsic – or external – motivation.

Extrinsic motivation will work for short periods of time, and for tasks that are repetitive. Extrinsic motivation requires that an external motivator is constantly applied – which means you always need an external 'reminder'. Our role as parents and educators is to help our youth prepare to function successfully and independently. The last thing we need to do is to reinforce extrinsic motivators - because we won't always be around to reinforce things!

Aside from requiring constant external input, extrinsic motivation often back-fires and can actually become demotivating. In his book, Drive, Daniel Pink explains that extrinsic motivation works reasonably well when tasks require little to no thinking skills. But as soon as a task requires some thinking, extrinsic motivation begins to fail. People who succeed in work that requires even basic thinking skills are the people who are intrinsically motivated.

Success in a knowledge-based economy requires that we're internally motivated, that our drive to perform comes from within.

So should we follow our heads or our hearts?

Yes! Both! Don't get caught in thinking that you need to do one or the other.

It's better if we don't choose and bring them both! I'll leave you with these words from JT O'Donnell:

You're a 'Business of One' and you're going to be paid for delivering services. Your services need to be valuable enough that they justify the cost of you. So (our children must) understand some simple concepts of supply and demand and how we set price.

We can start to teach our children that the best way to be worth more money and be more in demand is to solve a problem or alleviate a pain that is very important to your company. Career satisfaction comes from... solving problems and it has to be something that you're passionate about and care about. When you have those two, the sky's the limit.

... Now, go find some problems you love to solve. (JT O'Donnell)

Make Genuine Connections

No (wo)man is an island. ~John Donne

Whether we're introverted or extroverted, we humans are social animals who require connection with other people. Our connections guide us and shape us. They provide support.

When it comes to personal and career success, I've heard our networks described as our biggest assets. When I was teaching at the alternative school, chats with students who were struggling often centered around their support circles (or lack thereof). For these students, the school's staff and other students became their supports (which is great until long breaks like summer holidays). Learning how to make connections is critical.

> *The foundation of pretty much everything... is being able to make genuine connections with people, to understand where they're coming from and to build rapport with people in person... To be able to get into someone else's world, that's really important (and) will work anywhere. (Scott Dinsmore)*

Our connections fall into different categories, and the kinds of relationships we have with different people vary. Learning how to operate in this myriad of social relationships is an important skill.

> *It's important that young people learn how to work with a lot of different people, different age groups, different personality styles, etc... They tend to not get as much training in that area about what to expect. They're usually close to their peers so they're very comfortable working with people their own age but often times they are not as comfortable working with adults.*

> *Parents in this generation have tended to treat their children like equals and when these young people get into the work environment they don't find it to be the same format. I think it is really important to teach your kids basic communication skills and be cognitive of the rules of engagement in the workplace just to help them so they*

*don't get embarrassed and they don't make a major
mistake. (JT O'Donnell)*

Remember earlier in the book when Alexandra Levit
spoke about seeing a group of teens on a school trip sitting
in the airport texting each other and not speaking? She
had a greater insight into the impact that this can have
when students begin looking for work. The inability to
connect face-to-face with others can have significant
repercussions:

> *When you see them come and do their first interview, it's a
> disaster because interview communication is even more
> sophisticated than regular everyday communication. And,
> if you can't do the former you're certainly not going to be
> able to do the latter. The ability to make conversation, to
> show interest in other people's lives, to read people's body
> language, to assess what's meant versus what was said...
> I mean, these are things that sound basic but people in
> that millennial age, (born between the) 1980s and 95, they
> just don't have it as much and I would love to see them
> get a little bit better at that. Practice makes perfect.*

Making genuine contacts is a function of being able to
listen and show empathy for people. It's about turning your
focus onto the needs of others, and in being able to share
your own successes and difficulties positively and
effectively with others.

We can develop these skills by finding opportunities to
participate in activities that involve people from different
age groups. Finding work or volunteer placements or
mentoring opportunities for younger children all help.
Volunteer and mentoring opportunities can often be
accessed through school. Support your young adult's
participation in these events by asking about them at the
school.

Stick To It & Be Resourceful

HOW can I do this? Rumeet Billan

Rumeet Billan spoke to me about how to reframe difficult problems and how to ask the right questions. Instead of asking, 'Can I do this', it's more effective if we start asking, 'HOW can I do this'? This new question is critical for us to start asking ourselves if we're to develop what teachers call 'stick-to-it-iveness'. Indeed, this is a skill that was much talked-about during my teacher training – and a lack of 'stick-to-it-iveness' comes up in conversation with career experts as well!

> *Persistence, and the searching for alternatives (are critical success skills); in the business world you are not expected to just try, you are expected to keep on until you succeed. So when one thing doesn't work, try another. Job-hunters, for one, give up way too easily and way too soon, these days. (Dick Bolles)*

Dick Bolles isn't the only career expert who talks about giving up too easily:

> *One other thing that I heard of a lot feedback from companies hiring young people today is that many young people aren't very resourceful. They want a lot of instruction and they only do exactly what they were told to do. You're getting paid to solve a problem, alleviate a pain, figure out a solution so if I don't give you all the tools that you need to figure it out, go be resourceful. Find tools for yourself, find the answers, come to me with the solutions not the just the problems or the road blocks that you had; work through them.*

> *We see a lot of situations where young people don't get something done and the employer comes to them and they say 'I couldn't get it done.' 'Okay, well why didn't you tell me?' (The employee) said, 'Well, you didn't ask'. (The employee) didn't understand the deadline thing. That's just one other area I've heard feedback on. (JT O'Donnell)*

These are skills that come with repeated practice and support. Shifting our perspective from 'can I do this' to 'HOW can I do this helps us start to take responsibility and initiative. 'Stick-to-it-iveness' requires some confidence to begin, but it helps build self-confidence. It reinforces the belief that failure is just one more step on a road that leads to success.

> *My background is as a journalist, I'd say one of the key skills they teach you is how to be resourceful. When you run into a wall, (you ask), 'What are you going to do now that you're at deadline? Where are you going to find the information?'*
>
> *It taught us to think quickly and I think of all the skills that have served me well it's that I'm resourceful. I never see anything as a dead end; it's always, 'Where can I go next? What can I try next? What can I do next?' I never just sit and spin my wheels; I'm always trying something.*
>
> *There's a body of research that talks about fail fast, fail often. Because the quicker you do that the quicker you'll find the solution, the quicker you'll find something that works.*
>
> *A lot of people I know who were out of work were doing nothing more than sitting at a computer hours a day and sending out mass resumes to people. That didn't work for the first week, it didn't work for the second week; it wasn't working 6 months later. But they never changed the strategy.*

Success requires not just sticking to something and doing the same thing over and over again. It requires making changes when things aren't working. Einstein's definition of insanity is in doing the same things over again and expecting a different result.

Success requires sticking to a problem AND being resourceful.

Be Positive and Effective On Social Media

The rapid onset of the use of technology is what we often think when trying to pinpoint the defining characteristic of the Millennials. Most of us in the 'parents' and 'educators' categories aren't digital natives. We remember a time before the Internet, smart phones and texting.

Learning how to function online and in social media spaces requires time and energy, which is why many digital 'non-natives' are still hesitant to get fully on-board, but it's our responsibility as parents and educators to be in these spaces.

We're all too aware of how access to the Internet and instant messaging can amplify the negative aspects of our relationships. For example, cyber-bullying is an important social issue, but it's not a completely new phenomenon. Bullying existed prior to the technological revolution and it's become amplified as we all have 24/7 access to technology. If digital non-natives aren't in this space, then our youth are there unsupervised. This is why it's critical that parents and educators are become much better versed in, and use, tech tools.

Social media has changed how we interact and communicate. It's changed how we look for work as well as how we do work. To guide our kids effectively for life/work success, we need to have an understanding of how we are all expected to operate online. WE need to be operating online.

It's easy for those of us who are older to see drastic change and immediately become critical of those who embrace the change, without stopping to question our own fears and motives. One of the areas we find it easiest to be critical of is online behavior. Social media is now often blamed for changing the norms of behavior:

If anything, I applaud for Gen-Y's for being more open and honest; because they have to be now. We say, 'That's inappropriate that you did this or you said that'. Well, guess what? That's how all of (us) are in real life, (we) just pretend not to be.

Hopefully, we can get to a point where we can actually reconcile public versus private personas. (Dr. Woody)

We live in a time when there seems to be an erosion of privacy. There's not as clear a demarcation between work and the rest of our lives. We bring more of ourselves to our work and our workplaces as fewer of us work in strict 9-5 jobs. This may still seem more natural to youth than it does for many parents.

But this is changing quickly.

Having a positive and compelling online presence is important for all of us as job hunters who will find ourselves sourcing work opportunities frequently over the course of our lives. I like to remind people that there are two words in the phrase 'social media'. Youth might feel comfortable with the 'media' part of the phrase, but they more than ever require guidance learning the nuances of the meaning of 'social', especially in a hyper-active online world. It might be new to us digital non-natives, but we're the ones with a responsibility to help make sense of the changes and help our kids navigate the online world.

Those of us Gen-Xers and Boomers who aren't digital natives often need to get over our fears about the technology, and be more open to learning about the implications of the technology. Social media and other technologies aren't stand-alone entities - they're critical communication tools. Like basic literacy, technological literacy is a requirement of functioning effectively in the world. If we can't use the tool effectively, other aspects of our lives suffer.

We put blinders on. A lot of people who lost their jobs and stayed unemployed for a long time. A couple of their problems were:

(1) They were in an industry that was fading fast and had done nothing to position themselves to do anything else.

(2)They had no network. They had not kept up online. They thought LinkedIn and Facebook and Twitter were ridiculous and for teenagers. They went to industry conferences sometimes but didn't really network.

(3) They didn't keep their skills up so that they were transferable to other industries.

All those things hit at one time when you had thousands of people looking for jobs. Those people who had not positioned themselves correctly over all those years, ultimately, paid a big price for it. (Anita Bruzzese)

Social media platforms like LinkedIn, Facebook and Twitter aren't just ridiculous places for teenagers – people are there. If your goal is to connect with people to source 'how to' information or find openings, you need to be where people are. This holds true whether you're keeping up with what your teen is doing or you're looking for a job.

Consider the positive aspect of Facebook. How easy would it be for a teacher to set up a Facebook page for their high school classroom and post updates on what's being done in class, and when projects and homework is due? How would that tool change the conversation at home? How much better would it be to know to ask specifically about the Science Fair deadline rather than the generic, 'what's new'?

Kids aren't the only ones who can use Facebook on their smart phones.

If you're a parent in need of help getting it set up, just ask your young adult.

It's All About Resilience

One of the things that all the entrepreneurs I've interviewed have in common... is they are incredibly resilient. They absolutely have had failures, they've fallen down, they picked themselves up and dust themselves off but they don't internalize or personalize. ~ Dr. Woody

Resilience is the ability to cope with stress and adversity. Most of the stories and advice in this book highlight an aspect of resilience in some way. 'Rolling with the punches' is one phrase we often use and hear that speaks about resilience:

...Things work out the way they work out and you have to roll with it. (Kelly Green)

You could be taking a conference call at 10 o'clock at night if it's 7 o'clock in the morning for somebody else and you just have to be willing to roll with the punches. (Alexandra Levit)

Some of the examples illustrated a lack of resiliency – holding on to old behaviors and beliefs that resulted in more pain in the long run.

They haven't learned resiliency. They haven't learned that they can embrace change and not be afraid of it. There's a much bigger issue at play there than the career issue; that's something in their lives they have to fix first. (Anita Bruzzese)

The career guidance suggestions in the book are about instilling aspects of resilience in our youth. Some of the suggestions are relatively easy to implement, but others require that we as parents and educators address some of the life/work success and resilience skills that we haven't yet developed.

By far the most common theme I heard regarding life/work success was about building resilience, and that parents need to let their kids fail.

This is a foreign concept to many of us in the Boomer and Gen-X age groups. How often have we heard the phrase, 'If something's worth doing, it's worth doing right?'

Somewhere along the way, we forgot that if it's worth doing, it's worth doing wrong until we get it right.

Doing it wrong is how we learn.

Be Open To And Encourage Failure

The biggest advice I have for parents is to let kids fail. ~ Alexandra Levit

It's critically important for future success that our kids experience failure and then learn how to pick themselves up and move forward without letting failure negatively impact their self-esteem. We need to let our kids fail, and know that failure is expected and something they can handle. They need to know that their actions have an outcome - good or bad.

I know that the way that the millennial generation has been raised is in a way that's been very protective. They've been shielded from a lot of life's little SNAFUs. We're going to have to experience it at some point and going off into their first job is the perfect time to do that. So, hands off. Don't call your kid's boss if you're not happy with the way your kid's being treated.

Helicopter parents who just hover over every aspect of their child's lives have impacted the degree to which the millennial generation has prepared for professional work because they have not been independent up until this point. So, let them have some independence! Hands off. Let them fail. That would be my biggest advice. (Alexandra Levit)

I worked as a high school teacher before moving into the career arena. My head is nodding up and down vigorously as I read Alexandra's advice. There are certainly times when it's appropriate for parents to intervene and help their young adult navigate difficult situations, but there are also many, many more times when parents need to let

61

their young adult work through things for themselves. By all means, be there beforehand and afterwards to discuss values and skills, but let your children learn how to be responsible.

A lot of parents don't realize in over-helping their kids they're implying their kid isn't capable. We do tell parents to let your kids fail because experiments never fail. The more you fail, the more you learn. A lot of these kids have not had the chance to scrape their knees so their failure becomes so much bigger and scarier. (JT O'Donnell)

Our kids absolutely need to be able to fly when they leave the nest. None of us learns to fly by having our parents do it for us. We learn by watching, trying, failing, getting picked up a few times and eventually learning how to do it for ourselves.

Instead of fearing failure, we need to learn how to embrace failure. Know that dealing with failure can breed confidence, resilience and success:

Part of resilience is the personality factor. That's the part of the package you show up with. Some people are naturally more resilient than others. Another part of the ingredient is life learning.

Entrepreneurs are not afraid to take chances and they're not afraid of losing because more often than not, they've come from a place where they've had loss so they're okay with it. They're confident enough in themselves that they can go bankrupt, lose their house, and find a way to get it all back again.

Summing It All Up: The 5 Key Questions

Our job is to learn how to create life/work success for ourselves in 'uncertain times and novel circumstances'. One of the key concepts I learned from speaking with Dr. Woody was to 'attack the premise of every question' or assumption. As I spoke with the experts interviewed here and pulled together their top recommendations for helping prepare our youth for life/work success, I realized that they were posing 5 key questions to help keep us aware and reflecting on our experiences. Success isn't found in final answers, but in keeping these questions front and centre in our awareness.

1. **Explore, Explore, Explore:** WHAT is the work you can't not do?

2. **Be Clear On Your Values:** WHY are you doing what you're doing?

3. **Understand Your Skills:** Are you showing a preference for PEOPLE, INFORMATION or THINGS?

4. **Bring Your Head AND Your Heart:** WHO are you?

5. **Be Resourceful:** HOW can you do this?

And finally, our job is also to remember that we can't make things perfect .

Parents and Educators: We can help our kids understand their strengths, skills and values. We can help them really explore work opportunities in the area of their interests. We can help them be resourceful. Our most important job as parents and educators is to help them develop and be confident in their ability to 'roll with the punches', especially those punches we can't predict. We can't make life painless, but we can make more resilient children and young adults by helping them embrace struggle and failure and come out stronger.

> *Let me tell you what we think about children: they're hard-wired for struggle when they get here. When (we) hold those perfect little babies in our hand, our job is not to say, 'Look at her, she's perfect, my job is just to keep her perfect and make sure she makes the tennis team by 5th grade and Yale by 7th grade.'*
>
> *That's not our job. Our job is to look and say, 'You know what, you're imperfect and you're wired for struggle, but you are worthy of love and belonging.' That's our job. Show me a generation of kids raised like that and we'll end the problems that we see today. ~ Brene Brown (From her TEDxHouston Talk)*

Let's promise each other as parents and educators that having kids who do it wrong means we're doing it right!

Students and Recent Grads: There is no perfect job. Creating life/work success is about understanding ourselves and figuring out how to use our strengths and skills to benefit a company - whether it's someone else's company or our own.

You will go out there and you will screw things up. You will apply for jobs and be turned down or never hear back. Perfectly good and nice people get fired. This is normal - the hard bit is learning not to take it personally - because when you do that you become paralyzed.

...And unlike previous generations, you ABSOLUTELY need to know what your strengths and skills are and how to market yourself effectively. This doesn't mean you create a fake persona - it means you learn who you are and what you have to offer and you get out there and connect with your people.

* * *

I'll leave you with a bit of homework my counsellor assigned me one week:

Get out there and screw something up.

If you're up to it, report back at

Facebook.com/TheCareerTutor

Thank You

Before you go, I want to say a huge 'Thank You' for purchasing this book and investing your time with me.

You could have chosen any of the other great books on careers or parenting teens, but you took a chance with mine. Thank you!

If you like what you've been reading, I'd love your help....

Please take a minute to leave a review for this book on Amazon:

http://TheCareerTutor.com/book-review

Your feedback will help me keep writing the kinds of books and programs that will help you and your young adults create life/work success.

About The Author: Beth Campbell Duke, 'The CareerTutor'

As 'The Career Tutor', Beth helps students and recent grads make the most of school, find a great job and create life/work success.

In a 'past life' as a secondary school educator, Beth engaged a wide variety of young adults in their education and future careers, regardless of area or level of study. She worked with students in modified, regular and advanced stream programming, and was honored to be selected to work with colleagues on the re-design of a 'Career and Academic Readiness' program for 'at-risk' students. A former principal and mentor describes Beth as an 'ethical educational leader', but in her estimation, the highest accolade came when she overheard one student telling another, 'just go and ask her, she'll explain it to you so you get it.'

Find Beth online on on Facebook.com/TheCareerTutor, Twitter and LinkedIn. Learn more about Beth's career products and services at TheCareerTutor.com.

www.ingramcontent.com/pod-product-compliance
Lightning Source LLC
Chambersburg PA
CBHW070848180526
45168CB00002B/994